Confirmed
in the Spirit

Authors
Sisters of Notre Dame
Chardon, Ohio

LOYOLA PRESS.
A JESUIT MINISTRY
Chicago

Journal

Cover Design: Judine O'Shea
Cover Illustration: Susan Tolonen
Interior Design: Judine O'Shea

ISBN-13: 978-0-8294-2127-9 ISBN-10: 0-8294-2127-0

Manufactured in the United States of America.

LOYOLA PRESS.
A JESUIT MINISTRY

3441 N. Ashland Avenue
Chicago, Illinois 60657
(800) 621-1008
www.loyolapress.com

RRD / Menasha, WI, USA / 08-09 / 4th printing

This Journal belongs to

Uriel Salinas

who is preparing to be confirmed in the Spirit.

Name of My Parish

Name of My Pastor

My Confirmation Name

Date of My Confirmation

Name of My Sponsor

Name of My Bishop

Welcome

This journal is a companion volume to *Confirmed in the Spirit,* and it is a valuable part of your preparation for Confirmation. Journal writing has been recognized for many years as a tool for spiritual growth. Entered into reflectively, journal writing will help you to grow in self-knowledge and to express your Christian faith with greater depth.

This journal provides three ways to deepen your experience. You will find pages that invite you to reflect on a particular aspect of what you learn and pages that highlight how service is integrated into the life of a Christian. Other pages are blank, for you to use for notes and other reflections. The final section of your journal is a place to keep photos, cards, and other mementos of this special time in your faith life.

Prayer As I Open My Journal

Loving God,

Thank you for the gift of the Holy Spirit in my life.

As I open my journal, quiet my mind and heart

so that I can hear the Spirit's voice within me.

May this special time of prayer help me to discover more

about myself, others, and you.

Amen.

Remember a time in your life when God felt close.

What are five words you would use to describe your experience?

_____

_____

_____

_____

_____

The Holy Spirit is like a _____ who . . .

MEDIATOR

CONSOLER

MEDIATOR

INTERCESSOR

COMFORTER

CONSOLER

_____

_____

_____

_____

_____

_____

_____

_____

_____

_____

Reflect on an opportunity you've had recently to help someone.

In what ways can you recognize the presence of the Holy Spirit in your act of service?

_____

_____

_____

_____

_____

_____

_____

_____

_____

I would willingly _____ to deepen my
relationship with Jesus.

    risk being made fun of

    volunteer at church

    attend a Bible-study group

    risk losing my friends

Write the action you would choose. What would it mean for your life right now?
Which one would you not choose? Why?

_____

_____

_____

_____

If Jesus came to you today and said, "I want you to be my disciple," what would you say?
Why?

_____

_____

_____

_____

_____

_____

_____

_____

Who are some people who have served you this past week?

_____

_____

_____

_____

What are some qualities of discipleship that you observed in them?

_____

_____

_____

_____

_____

DEDICATION

FAITHFULNESS

LOYALTY

Think of some ways you express your Catholic faith in your everyday life. How long have you been doing these things? Why do you continue? What are some new expressions you would like to try?

_____

_____

_____

_____

_____

_____

_____

What people, circumstances, and behaviors help your faith grow stronger?

_____

_____

_____

_____

Which ones pressure you to ignore your faith?

_____

_____

_____

_____

_____

_____

Decide on an act of service you will perform this week to help someone feel included.
After you complete the act of service, write your reflections below. What did you do?
How did it turn out? Would you do it again? Why? Why not?

_____

_____

_____

_____

_____

_____

_____

_____

Choose one of the Beatitudes and write it below.

_____

Who are two people you know or have read about whose lives give witness to this beatitude?

MERCIFUL

_____

_____

_____

_____

PEACEMAKERS

MEEK

RIGHTEOUS

Loving like Jesus

means making room in our hearts
for all people.

**For whom do you have trouble making room
in your heart? If my heart were larger I . . .**

_____

_____

_____

_____

**For whom does society have trouble making room in its heart?
If our hearts were larger we . . .**

_____

_____

_____

_____

PEACEMAKERS

MERCIFUL

MEEK

Name three organizations in your community that help others.

_____

_____

_____

Whom do they serve? What needs do they address?

_____

_____

_____

_____

_____

Fill in each of the blanks below with one of the Gifts of the Holy Spirit and then complete each sentence.

God, I need _____ to _____

God, I need _____ to _____

God, I need _____ to _____

Choose one of your sentences to use as a prayer starter.

_____

_____

_____

_____

_____

K

WISDOM   REVERENCE

UNDERSTANDING

Describe a difficult situation you have seen or read about in the news. Imagine that you have the opportunity to meet with those involved. Which virtue that you've learned about could help resolve the conflict?

_____

_____

_____

_____

_____

_____

OWLEDGE

COURAGE

WONDER AND AWE

RIGHT JUDGMENT

If you had to convince someone that service is an essential part of living a Christian life, what would you say?

_____

_____

_____

_____

_____

_____

_____

_____

_____

What's your favorite song at Mass? Write down the words you remember. What are these words trying to tell you?

_____

_____

_____

_____

_____

_____

_____

_____

_____

_____

Imagine yourself at Mass, going up to receive the Eucharist. What do you most want to say to Jesus? What do you imagine him wanting to say to you?

_____

_____

_____

_____

_____

_____

_____

_____

_____

_____

WALK WITH ME

HEALTH
CONFIDENCE
SHELTER
HAPPINESS
JOB
LOVE

One way we serve others is by praying for their needs. What are some needs of others for which you can pray? Write them below. Then spend time in prayer.

_____

_____

_____

_____

_____

_____

_____

_____

SIGN OF PEACE

LAYING ON OF HANDS

ANOINTING WITH OIL

How do the symbols of Confirmation help you understand the grace of the sacrament?

_____

_____

_____

_____

_____

_____

_____

_____

Do you think you are ready to be a witness to Jesus in the world? Why? Why not?

_____

_____

_____

_____

_____

_____

_____

_____

_____

What are three things someone your age can do to be more active at Sunday Mass? (example: join the choir) Choose one and pursue it in your parish.

1 _____

_____

2 _____

_____

3 _____

_____

Think back over this time of preparation for Confirmation. On a scale of 1 to 5, how would you rate your spiritual growth?

(not very much) 1   2   3   4   5 (more than I expected)

What surprises you most?

_____

_____

_____

_____

_____

_____

What excites me most about being a confirmed Catholic is . . .

_____

_____

_____

_____

_____

_____

_____

_____

SHARING JESUS' LOVE

JOYOUS

UNAFRAID

CREATIVE

FREE

HAPPY

What's the most important thing you've learned about yourself by serving others?

_____

_____

_____

_____

_____

_____

_____

_____

_____

_____

_____

My Mementos